THE BIGGEST COUNTRY HITS OF ▶ ▶ ▶ 1995

© 1995 WARNER BROS. PUBLICATIONS
All Rights Reserved

Editor: Carol Cuellar

Contents

THE KEEPER OF THE STARS

Words and Music by
KAREN STALEY, DANNY MAYO and DICKIE LEE

ANGELS AMONG US

Words and Music by
BECKY HOBBS and DON GOODMAN

Additional lyrics

When life held troubled times and had me down on my knees,
There's always been someone to come along and comfort me.
A kind word from a stranger, to lend a helping hand,
A phone call from a friend just to say I understand.
Now, ain't it kind of funny, at the dark end of the road,
Someone lights the way with just a single ray of hope.

(To Chorus)

THINKIN' ABOUT YOU

Words and Music by
TOM SHAPIRO and BOB REGAN

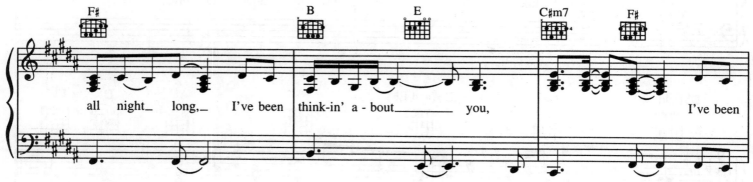

Thinkin' About You - 4 - 1

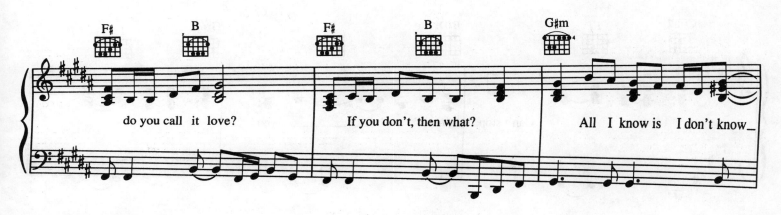

_what you've done,___ and this train of thought_ ain't a-bout to jump_ the track that it's on.___

Verses 3 & 4:

3. In the back of my mind, there's a se - cret place.___ But the whole world knows by the
4. _See additional lyrics_

smile on my face___ that I've been think - in' a - bout_____ you.

To Coda ⊕

Can't stop think-in' a - bout_____ you.

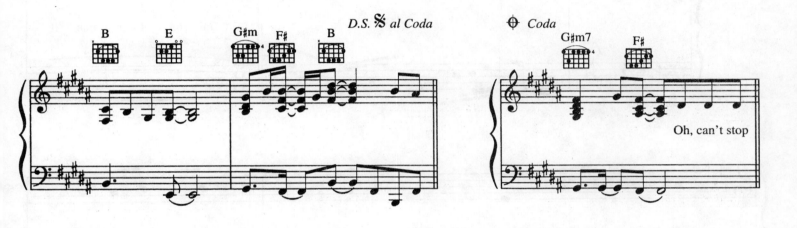

D.S. 𝄋 al Coda

⊕ *Coda*

Oh, can't stop

Repeat ad lib. and fade

think-in' a-bout__ you.__   I'm al-ways think-in' a-bout__ you.__   Oh, I do love

Verse 4:
I know it's crazy, callin' you this late,
When the only thing I wanted to say is that
I've been thinkin' about you,
Oh, just keep thinkin' about you.

SUMMER'S COMIN'

Words and Music by
CLINT BLACK and HAYDEN NICHOLAS

Fast country rock ♩ = 152

Noth - in' on Earth that - 'll get me hum-min' like a heat wave com-in'; I'll__ come run - nin', with her mak - in' that tan in the broad day - light,__ and ev - er - y night__ is a Sat- -ur-day night. And ev - ery - thing's__ right with the sum - mer com - in'; I'm the

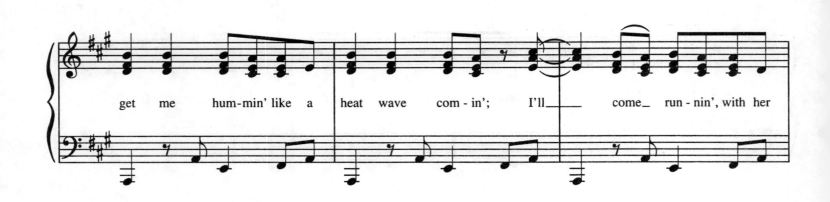

Verse 2:
When the day gets cookin', gonna grab my toys,
And it really doesn't matter which wave we're on.
Get to turnin' up them good old boys,
Crankin' into the night; by the break of dawn,
All the towns are red and I still see blond.
(To Chorus:)

AMY'S BACK IN AUSTIN

Written by
BRADY SEALS and
STEPHEN ALLEN DAVIS

Amy's Back in Austin - 5 - 1

22

Amy's Back in Austin - 5 - 2

To Coda ⊕

I bet Am - y's back in Aus - tin, and I'm

miss - ing her to - night.

Could this

Bridge:

des - ert wind car - ry me back a - gain? With my

Verse 2:
Workin' ten hours in a West Coast sun,
Can make the day so long.
Watchin' the moon crashin' into the ocean
Alone sure gets old.
I remember how sweet it was,
And where is she now, I need to know.
(To Chorus:)

AS ANY FOOL CAN SEE

Words and Music by
KENNY BEARD and
PAUL NELSON

As Any Fool Can See - 4 - 1

is know-ing I've been blind,___

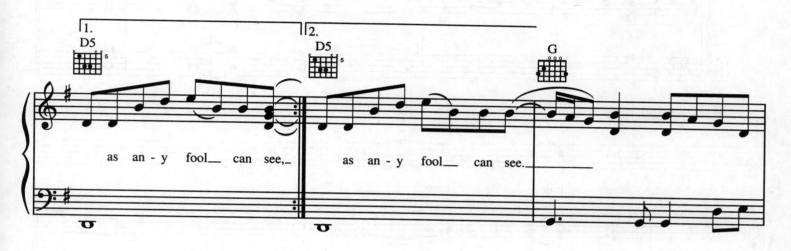

as an-y fool___ can see,___ as an-y fool___ can see.___

Verse 2:
How long did I think she'd stand
For me to be the kind of man
That came and went just as I dang well pleased,
While she sits at home alone
With fears and feelings of her own?
Lord knows goodbye would bring me to my knees.
(To Chorus:)

BABY LIKES TO ROCK IT

Words and Music by
STEVE RIPLEY and W. RICHMOND

32

Bridge:

boog - ie woog - ie woog - ie spread all o - ver the place,__ got it stacked to the ceil - in', got it

stick - in' in your face. You know my ba - by likes to rock it like a boog - ie woog - ie choo - choo__ train.__

2. John -   Ba -

Chorus:

- by likes to rock it.   Ba - by likes to rock it.

Baby Likes to Rock It - 5 - 3

3. She said her   Ba-   My ba-by likes to rock it like a

boog - ie woog - ie choo - choo___ train.___

Verse 2:
Johnny's in the back room suckin' on his gin,
Police are at the front door, screamin, "Let me in!"
Go-go-go-go dancer busy showin' off her chest,
She don't know what she doin' but she tries her best.
(To Bridge & Chorus:)

Verse 3:
She said her name was "Emergency" and asked to see my gun,
Said her telephone number was 9-1-1.
Got Brother Jimmy on the TV, Keillor on a stereo,
Said, "If you wanna get it, you got to let it go."
(To Bridge & Chorus:)

BUBBA HYDE

Words and Music by
CRAIG WISEMAN and
GENE NELSON

Bubba Hyde - 5 - 1

D7

Ain't missed a day of work in thir-teen years.__ He's a fire de-part-ment

G7   C7

vol-un-teer.__ He's got a yard that's al-ways just been mowed.__

G7

Col-lect-ed stamps since he was ten years old.__ You've nev-er seen a more__

D7   G7

reg-u-lar guy.__ But when the sun goes down on Fri-day night,_____

Chorus:
C7

N.C.

slaps on his Hi Ka-ra-te af-ter shave,__ puts on his El-vis jack-et,

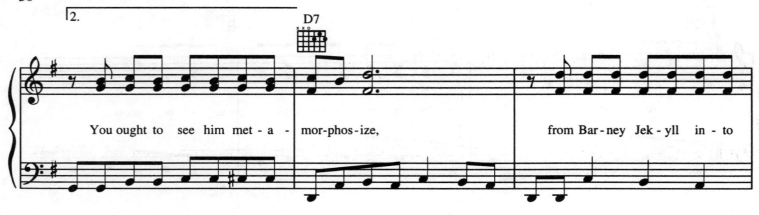

You ought to see him met - a - mor-phos-ize, from Bar - ney Jek - yll in - to

Bub - ba Hyde.

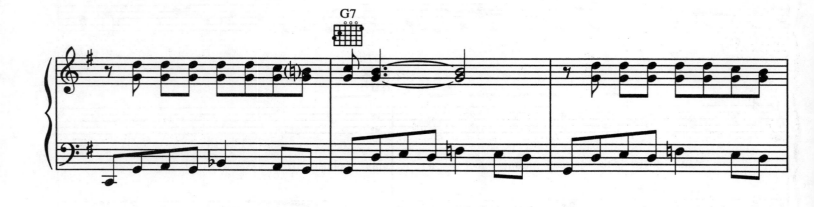

Instrumental solo ad lib.

Repeat and fade

Verse 2:
Monday morning it's a suit and tie,
Attention shoppers there's a two for one buy.
Tuesday afternoons he mans the wheel,
Makes his rounds in the bookmobile.
He's got a Wednesday night canasta game,
Thursday's the tourney at the bowling lanes.
His friends would freak out if they only knew,
The party animal he turns into.
(To Chorus:)

BETWEEN THE TWO OF THEM

Words and Music by
MICKEY CATES

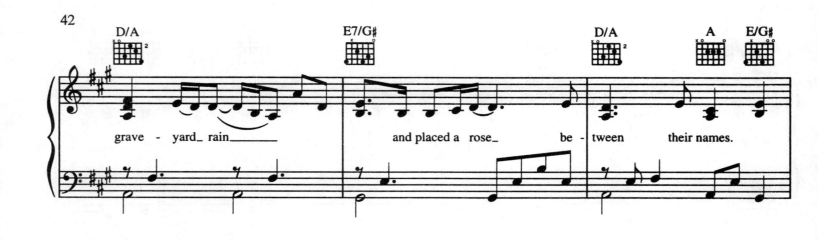

grave - yard_ rain_____ and placed a rose_ be - tween their names.

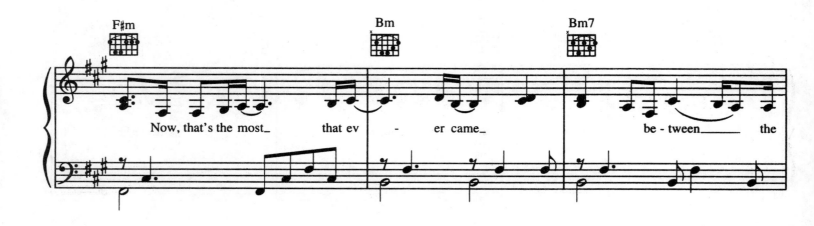

Now, that's the most_ that ev - er came_ be - tween_____ the

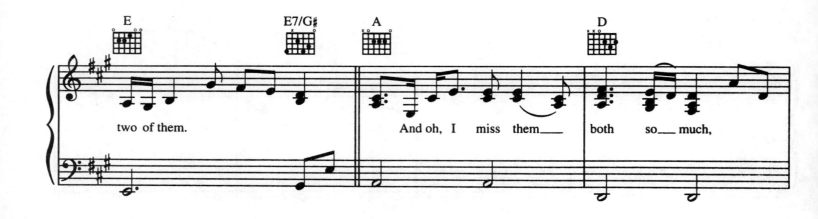

two of them. And oh, I miss them____ both so__ much,

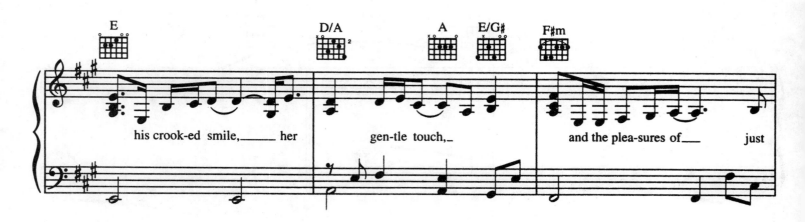

his crook-ed smile,____ her gen-tle touch,_ and the plea-sures of___ just

THE BOX

Words and Music by
RANDY TRAVIS and BUCK MOORE

The Box - 6 - 1

46

There was a let - ter ____ from ma -

ma ____ when she went out to Re - no ____ to

help her sis - ter out ____ in 'six - ty - two. ____

And a flo - wer from ____ Ha - wai - i; when

they went on ____ va - ca - tion, it was the first time that my

that was long— be - fore— we found— the box.

box. We all thought his heart was made—

— of sol - id rock, but

that was long— be - fore— we found— the box.

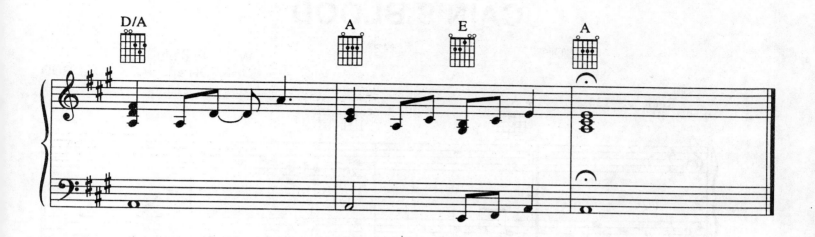

Additional lyrics

2. I guess we always knew it,
   But "I love you" was hard for him to say.
   Some men show it easily,
   And some just never seem to find the way.
   But that night I began to see
   A softer side of someone I had lost.
   I saw the love he kept inside the first time,
   When we opened up the box.

2nd Chorus: There was a picture that was taken,
   When he and mom were dating
   Standing by his 1944.
   And a faded leather bible
   He got when he was baptized,
   I guess no one understood him like the Lord.
   And a poem that he had written
   All about his wife and children,
   The tender words he wrote were quite a shock.
   We all thought his heart was made of solid rock,
   But that was long before we found the box.

CAIN'S BLOOD

Words and Music by
MICHAEL JOHNSON and JACK SUNDRUD

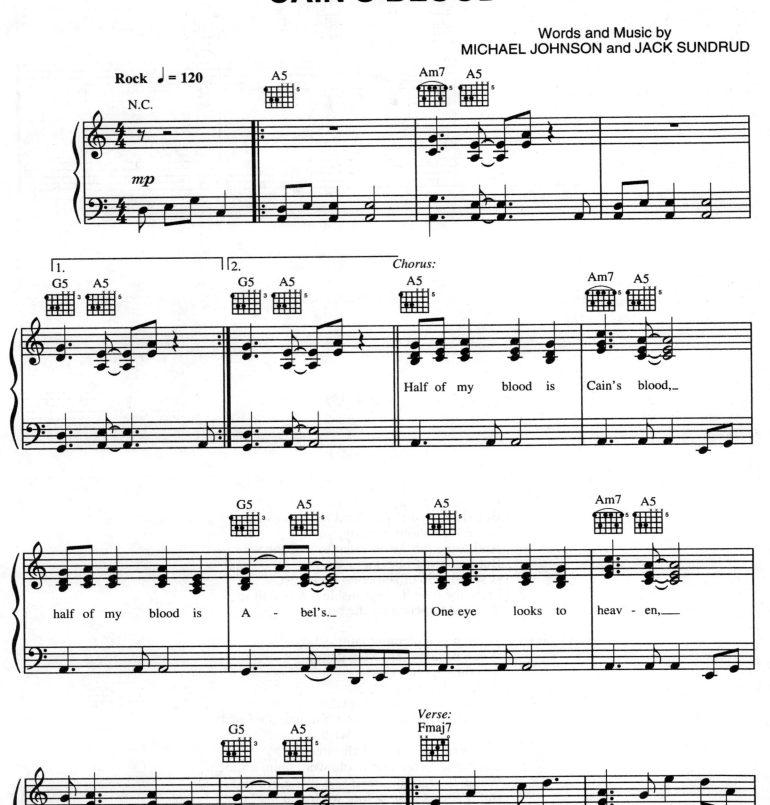

Cain's Blood - 5 - 1

52

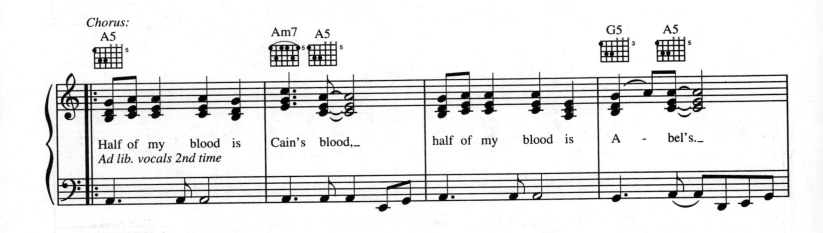

Half of my blood is Cain's blood,_ half of my blood is A - bel's._
Ad lib. vocals 2nd time

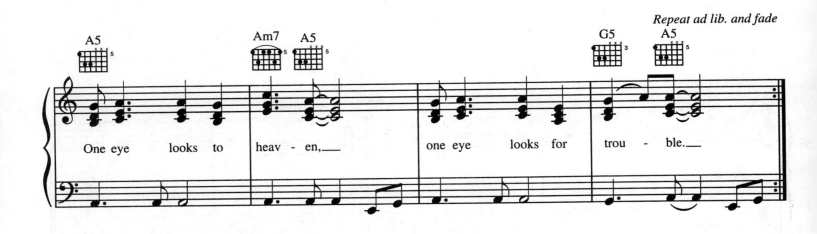

One eye looks to heav - en,_ one eye looks for trou - ble._

Verse 2:
Guess I always saw myself as a simple man.
But there's a man in the mirror I don't understand.
Every day I fight it, but I know down deep
It's the secrets I've been keeping,
Rising from their sleep.
(To Chorus:)

DEJA BLUE

Moderately ♩ = 104

Words and Music by
CRAIG WISEMAN and DONNIE LOWERY

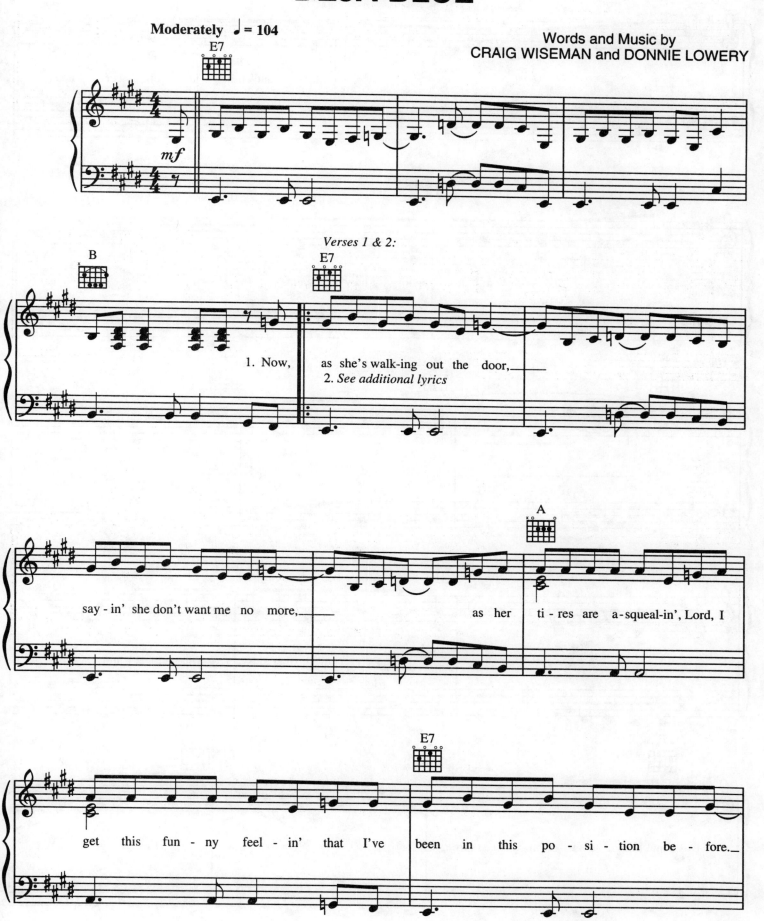

Verses 1 & 2:

1. Now, as she's walk-ing out the door,____
2. *See additional lyrics*

say - in' she don't want me no more,____ as her ti - res are a-squeal-in', Lord, I

get this fun - ny feel - in' that I've been in this po - si - tion be - fore.__

Deja Blue - 5 - 1

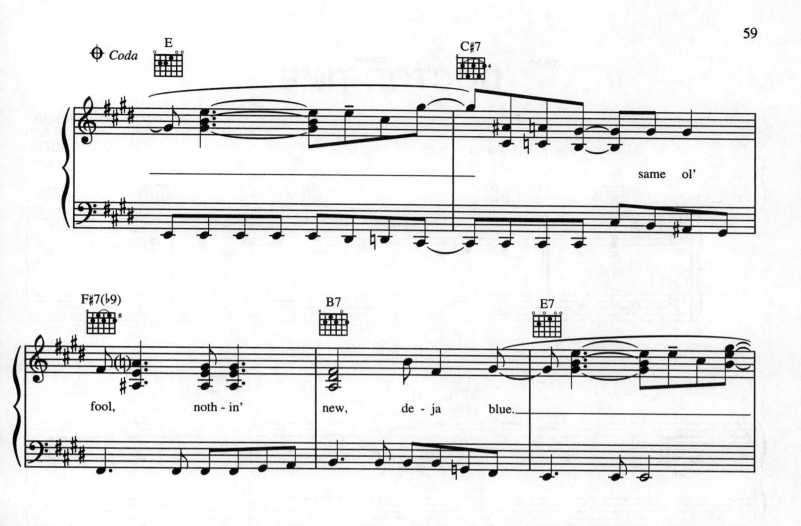

same ol'

fool,   noth - in'   new,   de - ja   blue.

Verse 2:
Now, it started in the second grade,
With little blondie what's her name.
Yeah, I toted all her books
And gave her long and gooshy looks,
But all she wanted was my brother Ray.
That first time nearly done me in,
But I've been there a hundred times since then.
(To Chorus:)

DOCTOR TIME

Words and Music by
LONNIE WILSON and
SUSAN LONGACRE

Verse:

1. May - be the juke - box can heal up a heart - ache,
2. *See additional lyrics*

but I'd go in - to debt._____ May - be the whis - ky can wipe out a mem - 'ry,

Doctor Time - 4 - 1

61

Doctor Time - 4 - 2

62

D.S. % al Coda

til I leave_____ this heart - ache in the dust.____ Doc - tor

Coda

through. 'Cause you're the on - ly one____

who can pull___ me through.

Verse 2:
Friends tell me hard work can fill up the hours,
But it don't fill this bed.
A quarter says a phone call can bring forgiveness,
She'd hang up again.
Gotta give me something to forget her
Everytime I lay down.
There ain't a night goes by I don't wish
I'd wake up a year from now.
(To Chorus:)

EUGENE YOU GENIUS

Moderate beat ♩ = 120

Words and Music by
LONNIE WILSON and BILLY LAWSON

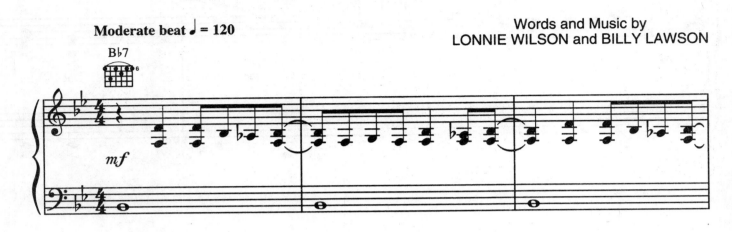

Verses 1 & 2:

1. Saw_____ you come through them_____
2. *See additional lyrics*

swing-ing doors,_ had_____ 'em hang-ing on ya, could-n't hold one more.

Eugene You Genius - 4 - 1

66

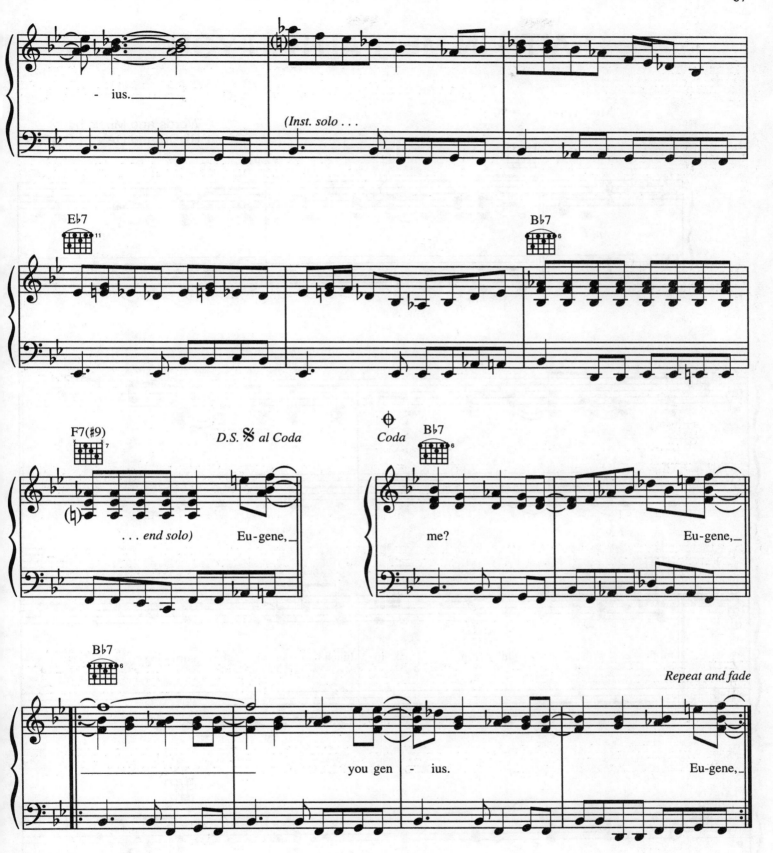

Verse 2:
It's more than the way you comb your hair,
That's making all the pretty girls stop and stare.
Tell me Eugene, I just gotta know,
Can I go down and buy it at the grocery store?
(To Chorus:)

FAITH IN ME, FAITH IN YOU

Moderately ♩ = 96

Words and Music by
TREY BRUCE and DAVE LOGGINS

Verses 1 & 2:

1. A single mother with two children, makin' lunches in the morning. And on her way to work she drops them off at school and tells them, faith in me,

Verse 2:
In the shadow of the city,
By the banks of the river,
From the doorway of his cardboard room,
He cries out faith in me, faith in you.
If over poverty and prejudice,
Over hunger and pain.
Over social injustice,
Just once let the voices ring.
Hear them sing, faith in me, faith in you.
(To Bridge:)

FALL IN LOVE

Words and Music by KENNY CHESNEY
BUDDY BROCK and KIM WILLIAMS

1. A lit-tle

Verse:

coun-try___ church___ on a two___ lane___ road,___ a bride and a groom com-ing
2. See additional lyrics

out the door._____ White___ lace dress and a red bou-quet, "Just___

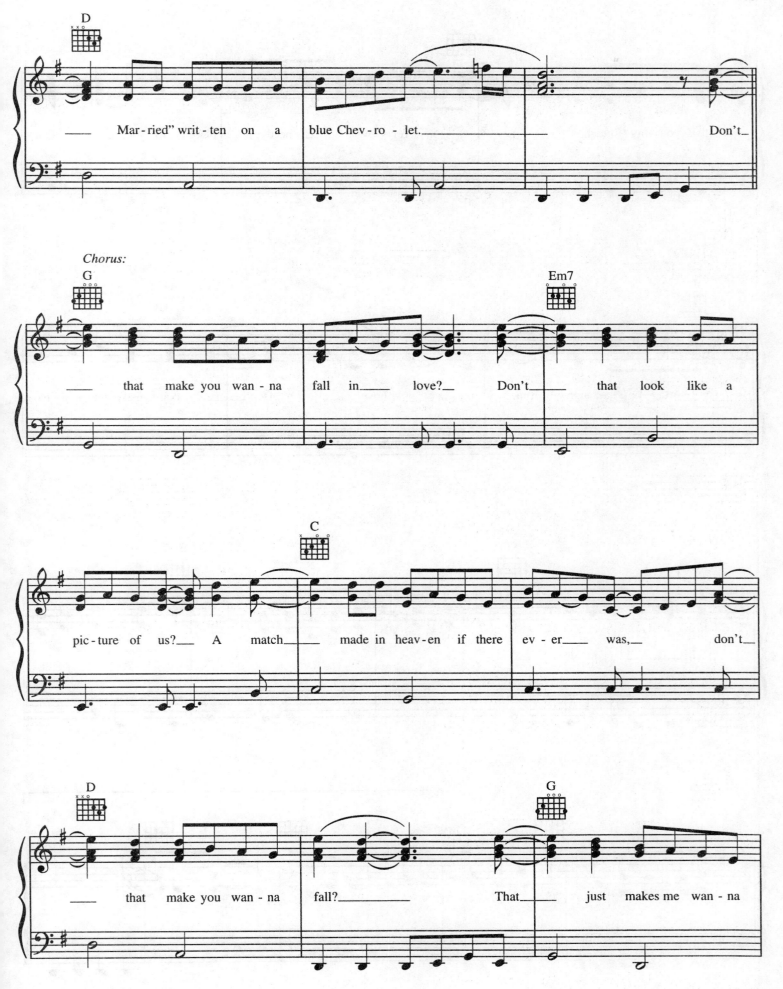

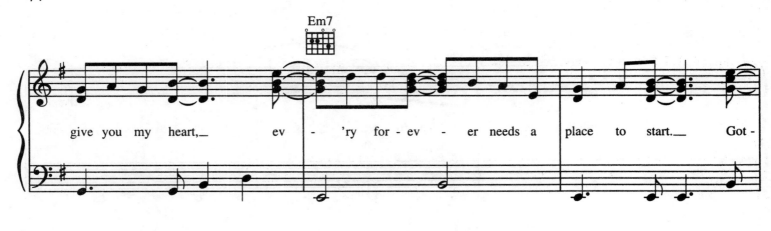

give you my heart,__ ev - 'ry for - ev - er needs a place to start.__ Got -

- ta be a sign from__ up a - bove._____ Don't____ that make you wan - na

fall_____ in love?_____

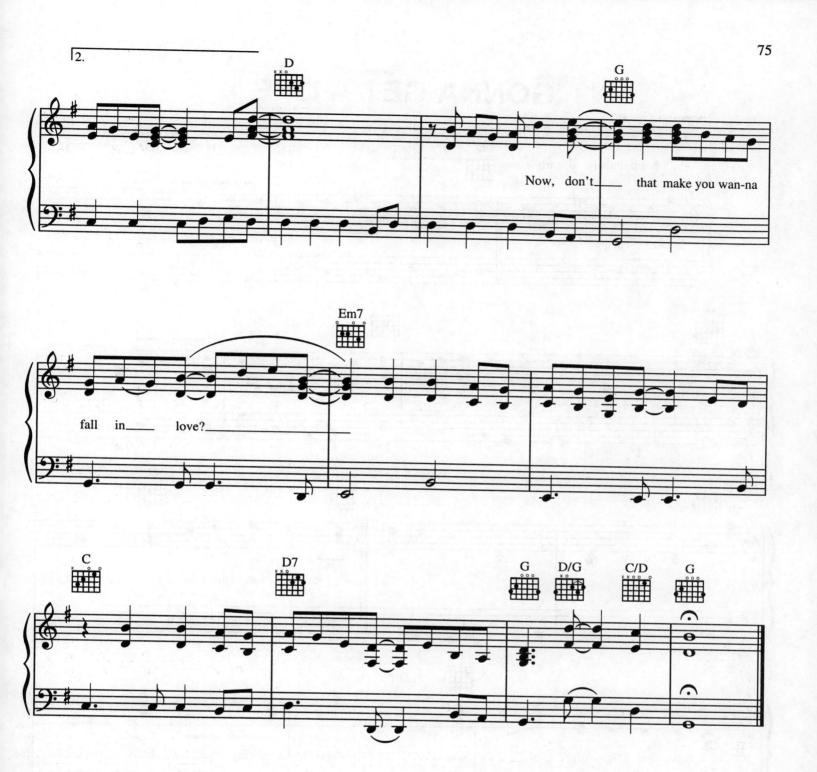

Verse 2:
Old folks sitting in a front porch swing
Still holding hands like they were sixteen.
Fifty good years, they're a lover's dream.
Darling, that could be you and me.
(To Chorus:)

GONNA GET A LIFE

Words and Music by
FRANK DYCUS and JIM LAUDERDALE

78

Gonna Get a Life - 4 - 3

be-fore the get-tin's_ done._

a tempo

Repeat ad lib. and fade

Verse 2:
This will be the last time you spin your wheels,
Leaving like a maniac.
You don't care about the way I feel,
There's no need in coming back.
(To Chorus:)

THE HEART IS A LONELY HUNTER

Words and Music by
MARK D. SANDERS,
KIM WILLIAMS and ED HILL

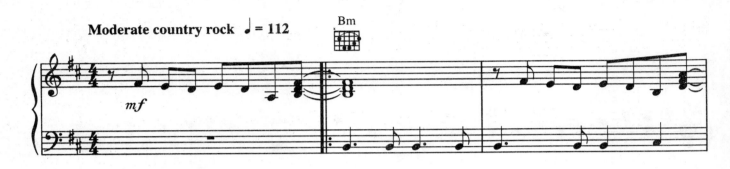

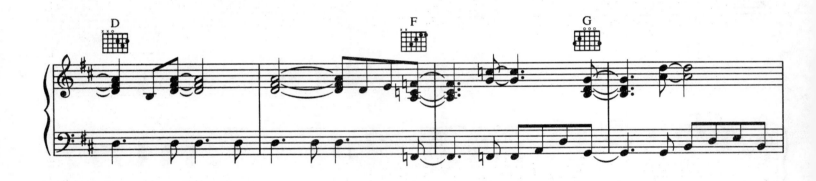

Verse:

1. She came in look-in' good___ and look-in' a-
2. She hears him say, "Hey, can___ I buy you a

The Heart Is a Lonely Hunter - 6 - 1

82

84

85

The Heart Is a Lonely Hunter - 6 - 6

HEART TROUBLE

Words and Music by
PAUL KENNERLEY

Moderately fast ♩ = 92

1. The

% *Verses 1-3:*

way you treat me, ba - by,   cheat and tell me lies.___   I
See additional lyrics.

guess I should-n't care___ at all,___ but still I sym-pa-thize___ 'cause you've got

Heart Trouble - 4 - 1

Verse 2:
You say that love can't touch you,
You feel no pain at all.
You think that you're above it, baby,
But I believe you'll fall.
'Cause you've got heart trouble coming on,
Yea, you've got heart trouble coming on.
Well, you'll get down on your knees, baby,
Begging me to come back home.

Verse 3:
You tell me you'll find someone else,
But no one's gonna care.
'Cause you have left a trail
Of broken hearts everywhere.
Now, you've got heart trouble coming on,
Yea, you've got heart trouble coming on.
Well, you'll know just how it feels, baby,
When you're left here all alone.

I AM WHO I AM

Words and Music by
TOM SHAPIRO, CHRIS WATERS
and HOLLY DUNN

I Am Who I Am - 4 - 2

A(9)
F♯m7
E
A(9)
B7sus
2. I've been
2.
A(9)
B7sus
E
A(9)
E
C♯m
___ I am who_ I am.
Inst. solo ad lib. . . .
B
A/C♯
B/D♯
Esus
E
A
E/G♯
F♯m7
E
. . . end solo
Bridge:
F♯m7
D(9)
E
A(9)
No re - grets,______ no a - pol - o - gies. I

I CAN LOVE YOU LIKE THAT

Words and Music by
STEVE DIAMOND, MARIBETH DERRY
and JENNIFER KIMBALL

I Can Love You Like That - 4 - 1

I GOT IT HONEST

Words and Music by
AARON TIPPIN, BRUCE BURCH
and MARCUS F. JOHNSON

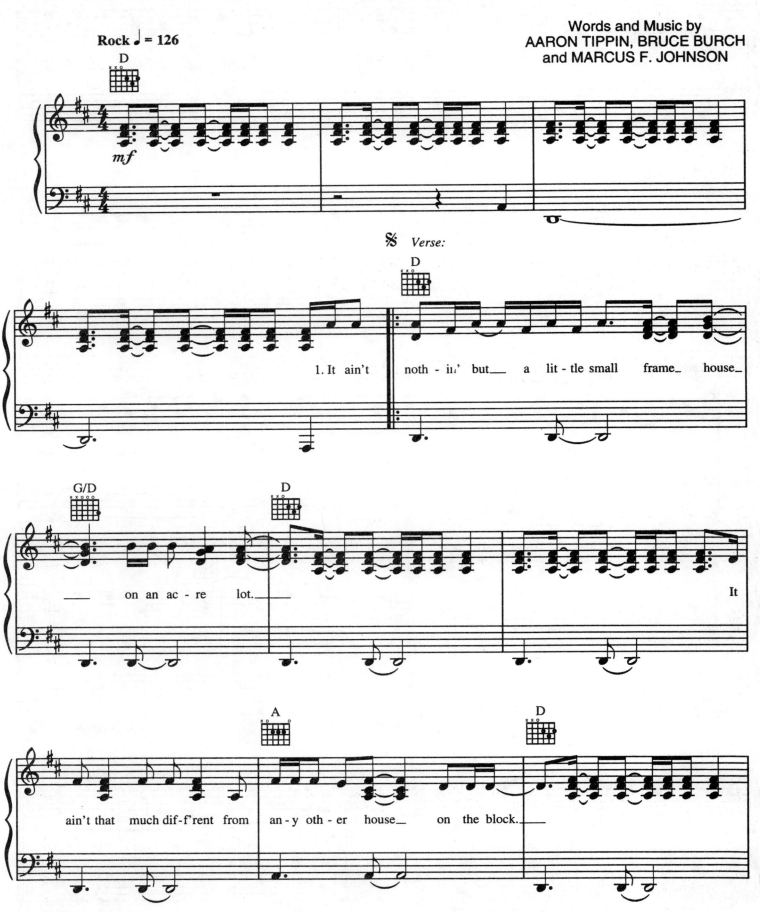

1. It ain't noth-in' but a lit-tle small frame house on an ac-re lot. It ain't that much dif-f'rent from an-y oth-er house on the block. It

I Got It Honest - 6 - 1

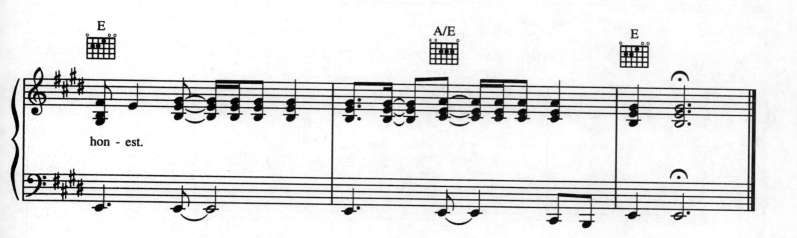

Verse 2:

Now, I roll out of the sack every mornin', head on down to the mill.
I give 'em all I got for eight, 'cause that's the deal.
If you check out my paycheck, well, you may find there ain't that much on it.
But every single penny I'm paid, I got it honest.
(To Chorus:)

Verse 3:

Now, you ain't lookin' at some dude that was born with a silver spoon in his mouth.
And I might seem like some kind of lowlife to that high-falutin' crowd,
But I'm plain spoken, straight talkin', and damn proud of what I have accomplished.
And some folks 'preciate that, some don't, but I got it honest.
(To Chorus:)

IF YOU'VE GOT LOVE

Words and Music by
STEVE SESKIN and MARK SANDERS

THE LIKES OF ME

Words and Music by
RICK BOWLES and LARRY BOONE

The Likes of Me - 4 - 1

110

No, you ain't ev - er been_ loved by the likes of me.__

Repeat ad lib. and fade

Verse 2:
If you need a helpin' hand to start over,
Baby, I can give you more than a shoulder.
You say you're having trouble believin'
That I won't be loving and leaving.
I say you've been hurt needlessly,
It's high time you were loved by the likes of me.
(To Chorus:)

LITTLE HOUSES

Words and Music by
MICKEY CATES and SKIP EWING

little white house____ in the heart of town,____ on a

2. *See additional lyric*

lit-tle side____ street,____ just a little run down, be-

Little Houses - 4 - 1

114

Verse 2:
Before too long, Sue and Bill
Were making plans for Jack and Jill.
Oh, happy day when the news came in;
But what to do? They found out Sue was having twins.
And when they could not pass each other in the hall,
Well, Sue would smile and say, "This place is really, really small.
But you know . . .
(To Chorus:)

LIVIN' ON LOVE

Words and Music by
ALAN JACKSON

Moderately

Two young— peo- ple with-out a thing say some vows and spread their
(See additional lyrics)

wings.— And set-tle down— with just— what they need— liv-in' on love.

Livin' on Love - 4 - 1

Additional Lyrics

2. Two old people without a thing
   Children gone but still they sing
   Side by side in that front porch swing
   Livin' on love.
   He can't see anymore,
   She can barely sweep the floor.
   Hand in hand they'll walk through that door
   Just livin' on love.
   (To Chorus)

LOOKING FOR THE LIGHT

Words and Music by
TIM MENSY and LIZ HENGBER

Verse 2:
At nineteen, I had all the answers;
Thought I could make it on my own.
As we were packing, she said don't ever forget
This is always your home.
Soon I found a one-room apartment
Has monsters of its own.
So sometimes I'd go out
And drive by that old house.
(To Chorus:)

NOT A MOMENT TOO SOON

Words and Music by
WAYNE PERRY and
JOE BARNHILL

Not a Moment Too Soon - 4 - 1

126

Not a Moment Too Soon - 4 - 3

D.S. %

soon.

Your sweet love saved me not a mo-ment too

(Half time) ♩ = 60

Repeat ad lib. and fade

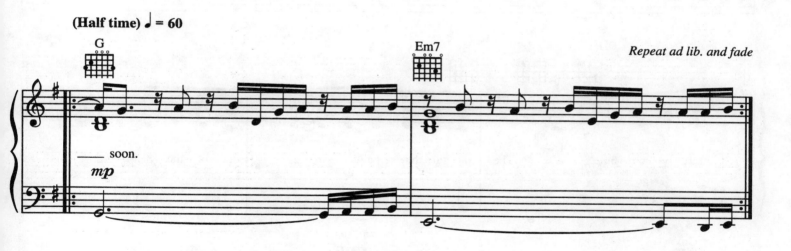

soon.

mp

Verse 2:
I used to think that love would never find me,
And the one who cares was lost somewhere in time.
But when you found me I knew I'd found forever,
You rescued me just before I crossed the line.
(To Chorus:)

THE RED STROKES

By
JAMES GARVER, LISA SANDERSON,
JENNY YATES and GARTH BROOKS

*L.H. tacet 1st Verse on recording.

The Red Strokes - 4 - 1

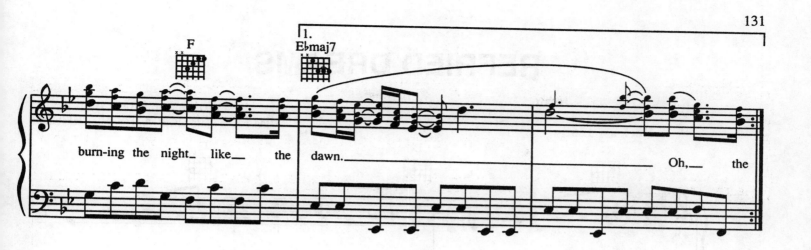

burn-ing the night_ like_ the dawn._____ Oh,___ the

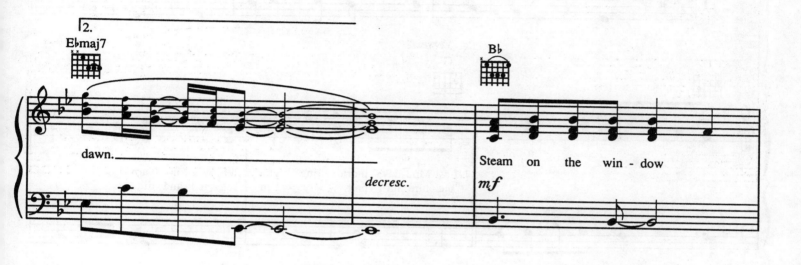

dawn._____ *decresc.* *mf* Steam on the win-dow

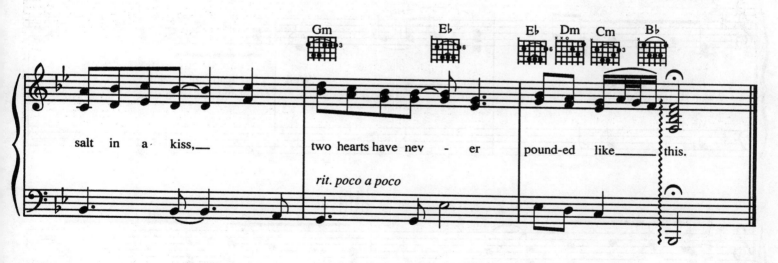

salt in a kiss,___ two hearts have nev - er pound-ed like____ this.

rit. poco a poco

Verse 2:
Steam on the window, Salt in a kiss:
Two hearts have never pounded like this.
Inspired by a vision
That they can't command,
Erasing the borders
With each brush of a hand.
(To Chorus:)

REFRIED DREAMS

Words and Music by
JIM FOSTER and MARK PETERSEN

134

SHE FEELS LIKE A BRAND NEW MAN TONIGHT

Moderately fast ♩ = 138

Words and Music by
AARON TIPPIN and
MICHAEL P. HEENEY

1. Her last ____ lone - ly tear-
2. *See additional lyrics*

drops fell ____ a - long ____ a - bout nine o' - clock. ____ His

She Feels Like a Brand New Man Tonight - 4 - 1

Verse 2:
Just like a kid in a candy store,
She's checking out the merchandise.
But she wants to find the keeping kind,
Who will keep her satisfied.
And he's gotta have a tender touch,
So if you fit the bill, brother, don't sit still.
Come on, step right up 'cause...
(To Chorus:)

She Feels Like a Brand New Man Tonight - 4 - 4

SONG FOR THE LIFE

Words and Music by
RODNEY CROWELL

142

Song for the Life - 4 - 3

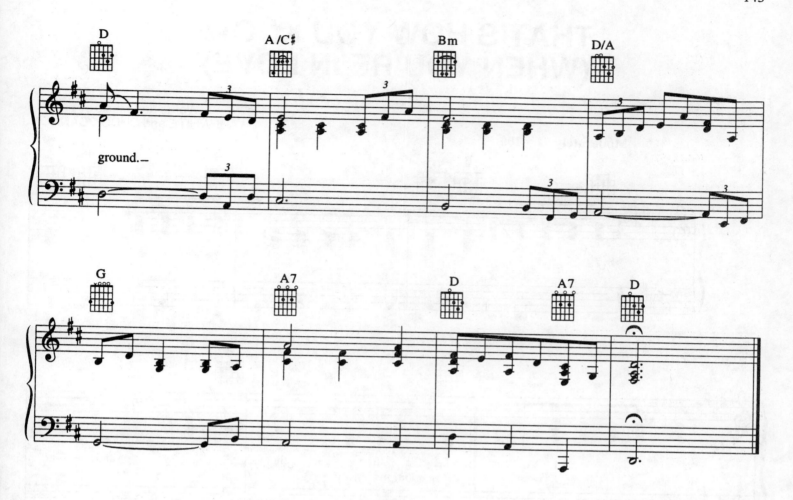

ground. —

Additional Lyrics

2. And the midsummer days sit so heavy,
   But don't they flow like the breeze through your mind.
   When nothing appears in a hurry,
   To make up for someone's lost time.
   (To Chorus)

3. Instrumental

2nd Chorus:
   And somehow I've learned how to listen,
   For a sound like the breeze dying down.
   In the magic, the morning is bringing,
   There's a song for the friend I have found.
   She keeps my feet on the ground,
   She keeps my feet on the ground.

THAT'S HOW YOU KNOW
(WHEN YOU'RE IN LOVE)

Words and Music by
LARI WHITE and CHUCK CANNON

That's How You Know (When You're in Love) - 4 - 1

Verse 2:
I had all but given up
On ever finding love,
Until I caught a glimpse of heaven
When I look into your eyes.
And your fingers touched my skin
Like a stormy summer wind,
Now I'm falling like the rain,
Oh, what a sweet surprise.
(To Chorus:)

THEY'RE PLAYIN' OUR SONG

Words and Music by
BOB DIPIERO, JOHN JARRARD
and MARK D. SANDERS

Moderately ♩ = 88

Verse 1:

1. Some-bod-y's at the front door, I can hear 'em knock-in'. Your
2. *See additional lyrics*
3. *Instrumental*

ma-ma's on the phone___ and she feels like talk-in'. There's chick-en on the bar-be-cue bar-be-cue - in'. Don't wor-ry 'bout it, ba-by, just drop what you're do-in'. 'Cause they're

They're Playin' Our Song - 4 - 1

Chorus:

play - in' our song__ on the ra - di - o.__ O - kay,___ Mis - ter D. J., at - ta

way to go.__ A mil - lion watts of love__ pow - er com - in' on strong.___ Dance__

___ with me dar - lin', they're play - in' our__ song.__

2. Oh the

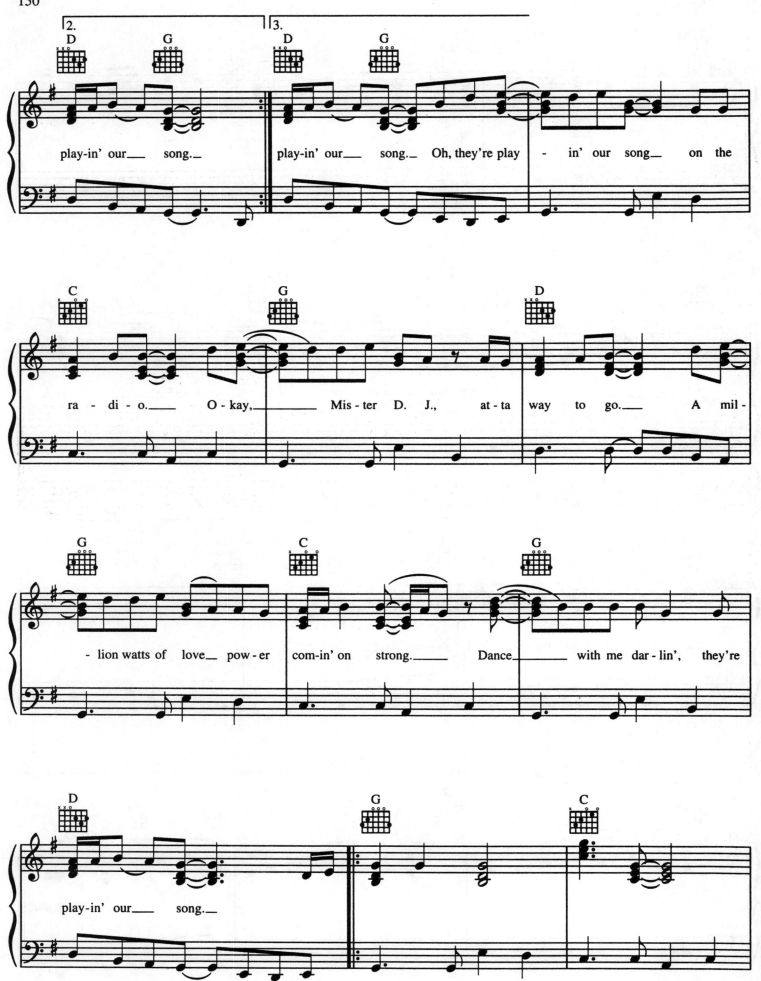

Repeat ad lib. and fade

Verse 2:
Oh, the house needs cleanin', the grass needs mowin',
We both got places that we need to be goin'.
Tomorrow's a big day, better get ready,
But tonight it's just you and me rockin' steady.
(To Chorus:)

THIS IS ME

Words and Music by
TOM SHAPIRO and TOM McHUGH

This Is Me - 4 - 1

154

This Is Me - 4 - 3

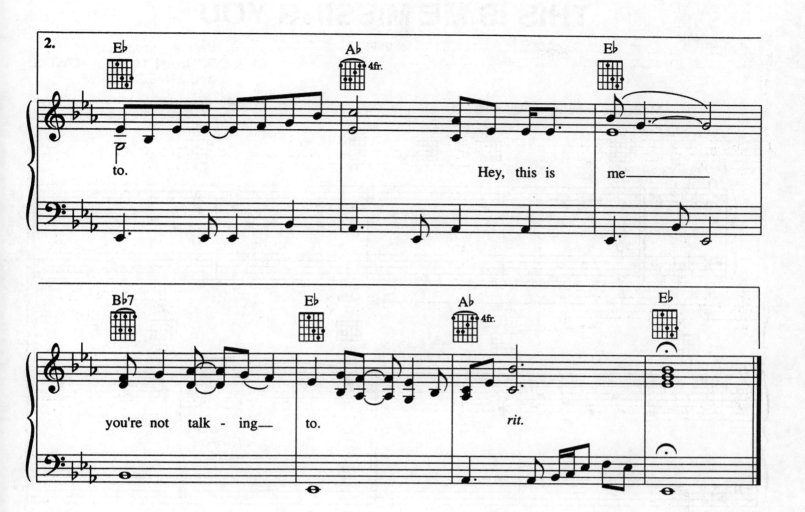

2. You can run to me no matter what you're running from.
If it's something I'm doing, I'll get it undone,
Just don't let me be a stranger to what you're going through,
Hey, this is me you're not talking to.

(To Chorus)

THIS IS ME MISSING YOU

Words and Music by
DEBI COCHRAN, MONTY POWELL
and JAMES HOUSE

This Is Me Missing You - 4 - 1

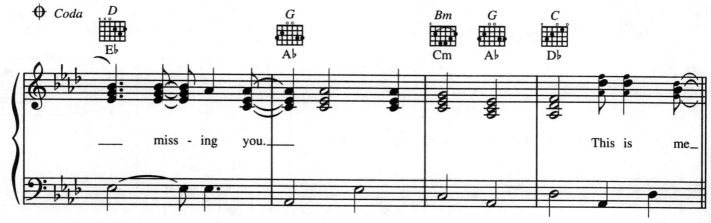

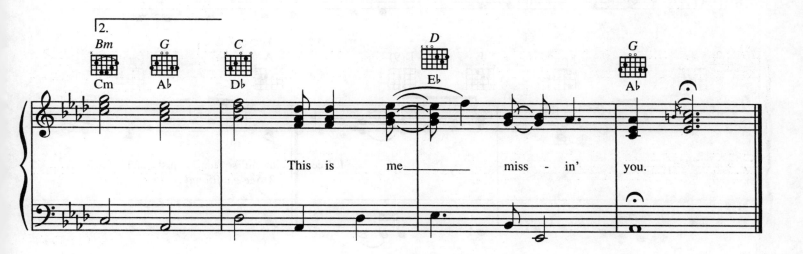

Verse 2:
If you see lonely
Clear skies turning stormy.
Lightning strikes and all you see is blue,
This is me missing you.
(To Bridge:)

Verse 3:
If you feel heartbreak,
Distant thunder like an earthquake.
If you wonder why the earth moves,
This is me missing you.

Verse 4:
(Instrumental solo)

Verse 5:
If you touch empty,
Reach in the darkness and don't find me.
Then you'll know just what I'm going through,
This is me missing you.
(To Coda)

THIS WOMAN AND THIS MAN

Words and Music by
JEFF PENNIG and
MICHAEL LUNN

This Woman and This Man - 4 - 1

Verse 2:
A stranger's eyes in a lover's face,
See no signs of a better time and place.
Have we lost the key to an open door?
I feel the need to reach out to you even more.
It's a circle goin' 'round.
If we don't get us out from under,
It's gonna take us down.
(To Chorus:)

TRYIN' TO GET TO NEW ORLEANS

Words and Music by
STEVE RIPLEY, WALT RICHMOND,
and TIM DUBOIS

Country shuffle ♩ = 132

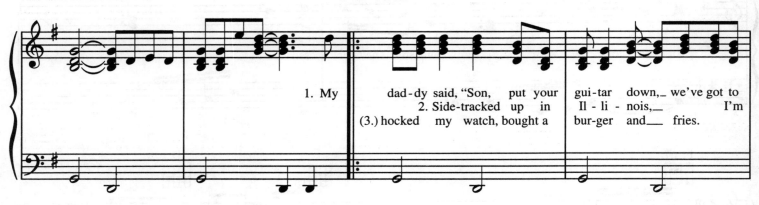

Verse:

1. My dad-dy said, "Son, put your gui-tar down,_ we've got to
2. Side-tracked up in Il-li - nois,_ I'm
(3.) hocked my watch, bought a bur-ger and_ fries.

build some fence,_ got to plow some ground."_ I told my dad-dy, "Try and un - der - stand,_ this
not that smart,_ I'm an in - no - cent boy. She called me "ba-by," she called me "hon - ey," she
Tried to pre - tend it was red beans and rice. Mid-night in Mem-phis, hel - lo to Grace-land,

(%) Instrumental solo ad lib. . . .

Tryin' to Get to New Orleans - 4 - 1

fe and Ca - jun queens. You know I need a lit - tle help, you see I'm

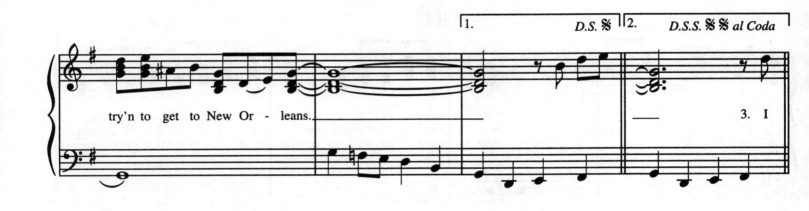

try'n to get to New Or - leans.   3. I

Yeah, I need a lit - tle help, you see I'm try'n to get to New Or - leans.

Well, I'm just an old poor boy, chas - in' down a dream. And I

UNTANGLIN' MY MIND

Words and Music by
CLINT BLACK and MERLE HAGGARD

Slowly ♩ = 69

(with pedal)

Verse:

1. I guess you're glad___ to see___ I'm fin - 'lly leav - in'. I know things for you___ will change now___ for___ the good. But it's all that I can do___ to pack my___

Untanglin' My Mind - 4 - 1

some - where un - tan - glin' _____ my mind.

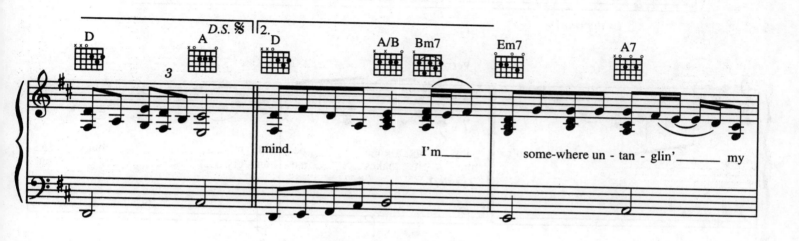

mind.   I'm_____   some-where un - tan - glin' _____ my

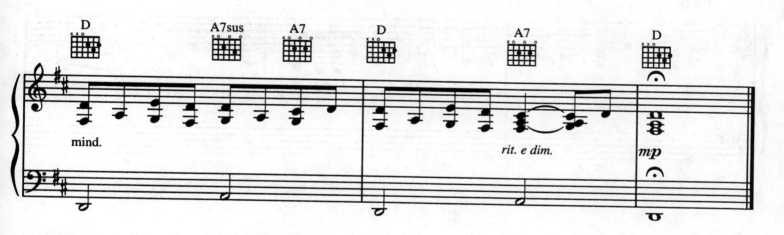

mind.   *rit. e dim.*   *mp*

Verse 2:
Tell 'em I won't be ridin', I'll be walkin'
'Cause I don't think a crazy man should drive.
Anyway, the car belongs to you, now,
Along with any part of me that's still alive.
But there's really not much left you could hold on to,
And if you did, it wouldn't last here, anyway.
It'd head to where the rest of me rolled on to,
So, even if I wanted to, I couldn't stay.
(To Chorus:)

WE CAN'T LOVE LIKE THIS ANYMORE

Words and Music by
JOHN JARRARD and WENDELL MOBLEY

We Can't Love Like This Anymore - 4 - 1

D7 G A D
I'm not sure we'd be this lone-ly by our - selves.
D7 G A
But I won't give up as long as there's a chance,
Bm F#m7 Bm G
so where we go from
C A Asus4/2 A
here is in your hands.
3. Just say it's
mp

WHAT MATTERED MOST

Words and Music by
VINCE MELAMED and
GARY BURR

Moderate country rock ♩ = 72

What Mattered Most - 4 - 1

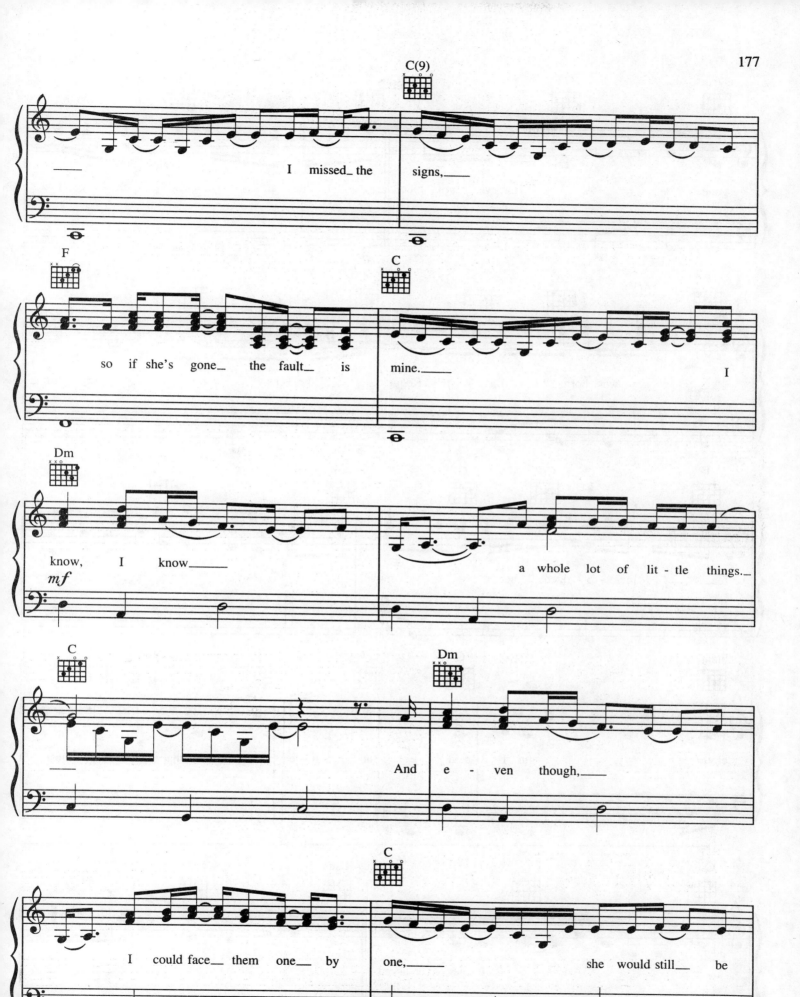

C/E   F   C/G   G

her hair is long,___ six - ty four,___ she was born___ in Ba - ton Rouge.___

C   C/E   F   C/G   G

___ Her fa-ther's tall,___ her mo-ther's gone,___ she moved out west___ when she was two.___

C   C/E   F   C/G   G

___ The way she laughed,___ the way she loved,___ oh my God___ what did I do?___

Repeat ad lib. and fade

C   C/E   F   C/G   G

Verse 2:
I never asked, she never said,
And when she cried I turned my head.
She dreamed her dreams behind closed doors;
That made them easy to ignore.
And I know, I know, I missed the forest for the trees.
Now all I have to show,
Or would she walk out the door?
The cold facts and nothin' more.
(To Chorus:)

WHEN LOVE FINDS YOU

Words and Music by
VINCE GILL and MICHAEL OMARTIAN

Love sure is
(See additional lyrics)

some-thing no one can ex - plain. It can

bring you such joy,—— it can bring—— you

When Love Finds You - 4 - 1

Additional lyrics

2. Love is the power that makes your heart beat,
It can make you move mountains, make you drop to your knees.
When it finally hits you, you won't know what to do,
There's nothing you can say when love finds you.

3. *Instrumental*
And when you least expect it, it will finally come true,
There's nothing you can say when love finds you.

WHO'S SHE TO YOU

Words and Music by
FRANK J. MYERS and DONNY KEES

fore I came a-long. I've of-ten won-dered who she was and

Chorus:

was she real - ly gone. Who's she to you? And

where does that leave me? Is she still in your heart or

just a mem-o-ry. If she said hel-lo, would

you tell me good - bye.___ Who's she to you?___

— And dar-lin' who am I?___

Verse 2:
The looks you're givin' her
Are doin' things to me.
You say there's no reason at all
For my jealousy.
But as long as there's a little smoke,
A fire's never cold.
If history repeats itself,
What does our future hold?
(To Chorus:)

YOU AND ONLY YOU

Words and Music by
CHUCK JONES and J.D. MARTIN

You and Only You - 4 - 1

Verse 2:
Happy ever after's not so easy to acquire,
Only you could ever measure up to my desire.
Baby, you gave up on me just a little bit too soon,
And left me here for lonely, howling at the moon.
(To Chorus:)

Verse 3:
I'm asking your forgiveness,
I know I'm the one to blame.
I've finally learned my lesson,
Love is more than just a game.
And please don't try to tell me,
A little time is all I need.
'Cause time, he ain't no friend of mine,
'Til he brings you back to me.
(To Chorus:)

YOU CAN SLEEP WHILE I DRIVE

Lyrics and Music by
MELISSA ETHERIDGE

* Melody sung 1 octave lower

Verse 2:
I'll pack my bag and load up my guitar,
In my pocket I'll carry my harp.
I got some money I saved,
Enough to get underway,
And baby you can sleep while I drive.

Verse 3:
We'll go through Tucson up to Sante Fe,
And Barbara in Nashville says we're welcome to stay.
I'll buy you boots down in Texas,
A hat in New Orleans,
And in the morning you can tell me your dreams.

WHEREVER YOU GO

Words and Music by
CLINT BLACK and HAYDEN NICHOLAS

Moderate rock ♩ = 116

Wherever You Go - 5 - 1

Wherever You Go - 5 - 3

Verse 2:

Bottle of scotch whiskey, whatever you find;
When you're out on the wire, it's a matter of time.
Changing every moment when you're taking the fall;
There's everything to gain when you're losing it all.
Feel your head spinning with your feet on the ground;
You climb the wrong ladder, and it's keeping you down.
Think you're getting higher, but you're still laying low,
You don't want to be anyone you know.
(To Chorus:)

WHOSE BED HAVE YOUR BOOTS BEEN UNDER?

Words and Music by
SHANIA TWAIN and ROBERT JOHN "MUTT" LANGE

202

Whose Bed Have Your Boots Been Under? - 5 - 2

Whose Bed Have Your Boots Been Under? - 5 - 3

Verse 2:
I heard you've been sneakin'
Around with Jill.
And what about that weekend
With Beverly Hill?
And I've seen you walkin'
With long-legs Louise.
And you weren't just talkin'
Last night with Denise.
(To Chorus:)

Additional lyrics for D.S.:
So next time you're lonely,
Don't call on me.
Try the operator,
Maybe she'll be free.
(To Chorus:)

GIVE ME ONE MORE SHOT

Moderately ♩ = 112

Words and Music by
RANDY OWEN, TEDDY GENTRY
and RONNIE ROGERS

Verse 2:
I could complain about taxes, or the weather that we're having.
Go on and on about things that are wrong from New York to L. A.
But it's just not my nature to sit around feeling sad,
We're only here for a little while, so why not smile.
Living ain't all that bad.
(To Chorus:)

HERE I AM

Words and Music by
TONY ARATA

Here I Am - 5 - 1

212

look-in' for me ev-er-y-where.___ And you know that you're gon-na find___ me if you keep on drink-in' fast.___ 'Cause, hon-ey, I'm right___ here wait--in' on___ you at the bot-tom of your glass. And

Chorus:

here I___ am,___ here I___ am,___

Here I Am - 5 - 2

214

Here I Am - 5 - 4

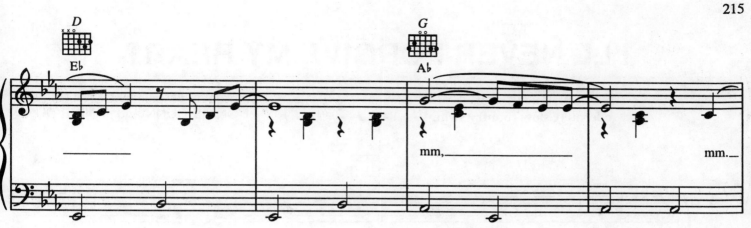

Verse 2:
It ain't workin' darlin', hard as you may try.
You keep hearin' the words you told me in everyone's goodbyes.
And you know that you're just one step from another one being gone.
I know I've seen 'em all unravel,
I've been watchin' it all along.

Chorus 2:
Here I am, here I am,
In every lie you're hearin'
That burn you just like a brand,
Here I am.
(To Bridge:)

Chorus 3:
Here I am, here I am,
I still carry a flame for you
Burnin' me like a brand,
Here I am.

I'LL NEVER FORGIVE MY HEART

Words and Music by DEAN DILLON,
RONNIE DUNN and JANINE DUNN

Moderately slow country swing ♩ = 84

I'll Never Forgive My Heart - 3 - 1

I'll Never Forgive My Heart - 3 - 2

I SEE IT NOW

Moderately slow country waltz ♩ = 96

Words and Music by PAUL NELSON,
LARRY BOONE and WOODY LEE

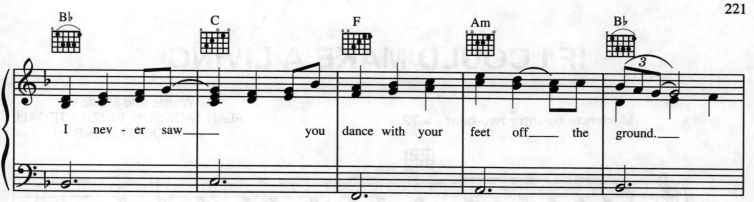

I nev-er saw_____ you dance with your feet off____ the ground.____

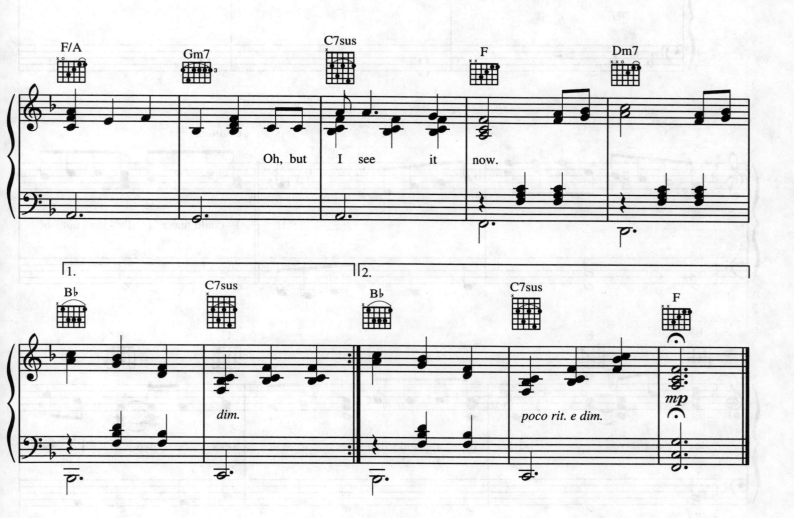

Oh, but I see it now.

dim.

poco rit. e dim.

mp

Verse 2:
Holding him, you never looked more beautiful.
Letting go has been so hard on me.
And sitting here it's clear to see what he means to you.
The way you look at him it ain't no mystery;
He's all I couldn't be.
(To Chorus:)

IF I COULD MAKE A LIVING

Words and Music by
ALAN JACKSON, KEITH STEGALL
and ROGER MURRAH

lov - ing___ you.

Verse:

1. Ear - ly ev - 'ry morn-ing when the
2. *See additional lyrics.*

sun comes up___ I'm punch-in' that clock_ on the wall; break-in' my back just to

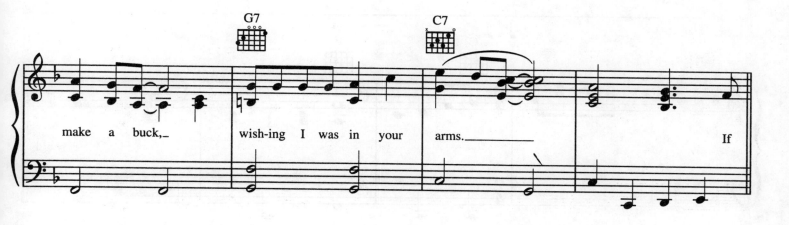

make a buck,_ wish-ing I was in your arms._____ If

Chorus:

I could make a liv-ing out of lov-ing you,_ I'd be a mil-lion-aire in a

224

week or two.___ I'd be do-ing what I love and lov - ing what I do___ if

I could make a liv-ing out of lov-ing___ you.

2. I could

If I Could Make a Living - 5 - 3

week or two.___ I'd be do-ing what I love and lov - ing what I do___ if

I could make a liv - ing out of lov - ing___ you.

Verse 2:
I could work all day and feel right at home
Loving that 8 to 5,
And never have to leave you here alone
When I'm working over-time.
(To Chorus:)

LOOK WHAT FOLLOWED ME HOME

Words and Music by
TOMMY POLK and DAVID BALL

Verse 2:
Well, I walked down to the river at the break of dawn
With a picture of you, darling, up underneath my arm.
I said, "The heartache's over, today is your last day."
And I thanked that muddy river as it carried you away.
(To Chorus:)

MAYBE SHE'S HUMAN

Words and Music by
KENT ROBBINS & LAYNG MARTINE, JR.

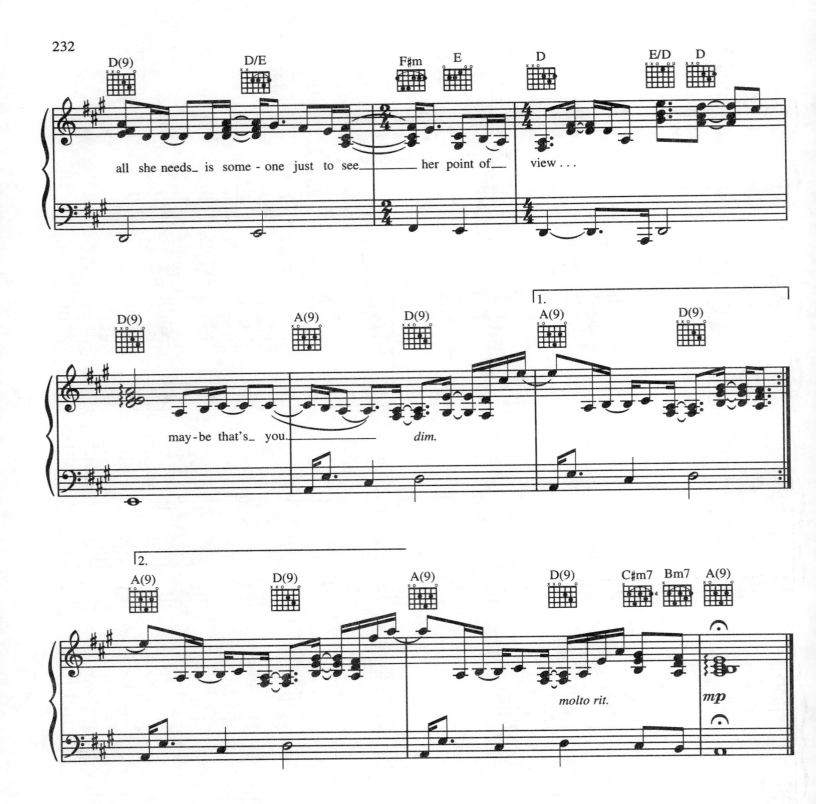

Verse 2:
After working late today, she brings in bags of groceries,
Bandages a skinned-up knee as the chicken starts to fry.
She drops a glass, the baby cries, the phone rings,
That's when you walk in, unloading all your problems
And the worries on your mind.
When you mention it's your "boys' night out," she tears you into shreds.
And you just can't quite figure why she gets so upset.
(To Chorus:)

MI VIDA LOCA
(MY CRAZY LIFE)

Words and Music by
PAM TILLIS and JESS LEARY

Mi Vida Loca - 5 - 1

234

Chorus:

Mi vi-da lo-ca,___ o-ver___ and o-ver.___ Des-tin-y turns on___ a dime.___

I go where___ the wind blows,___ you can't tame___ a

wild rose.___ Wel-come___ to my cra-zy life.

Mi Vida Loca - 5 - 2

2. Sweet - life.

236

Verse 2:
Sweetheart, before this night is through,
I could fall in love with you.
Come dancin' on the edge with me,
Let my passion set you free.
(To Chorus:)

SOUTHERN GRACE

Written by
PORTER HOWELL, BRADY SEALS
and STEWART HARRIS

Verse 2:
You should see the way she walks into a room;
It's almost like her feet don't touch the floor.
But when the chips are down, her feet are firmly on the ground.
I could never ask for any more.
(To Chorus:)

STAY FOREVER

Words and Music by
BENMONT TENCH and HAL KETCHUM

244

Stay Forever - 3 - 2

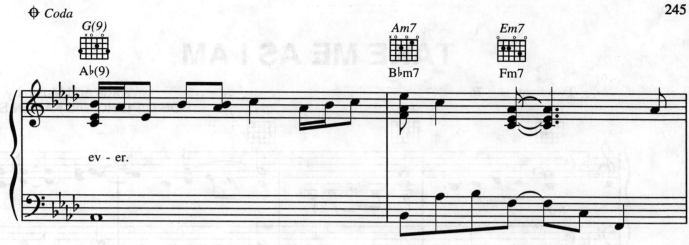

Verse 2:
Maybe I care too much,
Maybe I'll push you away.
Maybe I'd have my doubts,
If I were in your place.
And if you could see inside
This aching heart of mine,
Maybe you would stay forever.
(To Bridge:)

Verse 3:
And if you would trust in me
And this love of mine,
We'll sail an endless sea
Under a starry sky.
And when the cold wind blows,
We'll hold each other close,
Maybe you will stay forever.

Verse 4:
Instrumental solo . . .
And when the cold wind blows,
We'll hold each other close.
Maybe you will stay forever.

TAKE ME AS I AM

Two beat ♩ = 76

Words and Music by
BOB DIPIERO and KAREN STALEY

Gm7
Bb(2)
C7
not just prom - is - es and emp - ty fan - ta - sies. I don't
...end solo)
Chorus:
F
Bb
F/Bb
Dm7
C
need a bed of ros - es, 'cause
F
Bb
Dm
C
ros - es with - er a - way. All I
F
Bb
Dm7
C
real - ly need is hon - es - ty
Bb(2)
from some-one with a strong heart, a gen - tle hand,

Verse 2:
Baby, I need for you to know
Just exactly how I feel.
Fiery passions come and go.
I'd trade a million pretty words
For one touch that is real.
(To Chorus:)

TILL YOU LOVE ME

Words and Music by
BOB DIPIERO and GARY BURR

Till You Love Me - 3 - 1

so I'll do all that I can to catch that ghost of a chance._____ The

cresc.

Chorus:

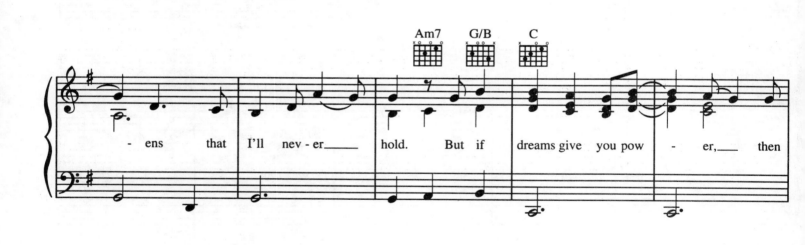

sun-light, the moon-light are be-yond my con-trol._____ And there are stars in the heav-

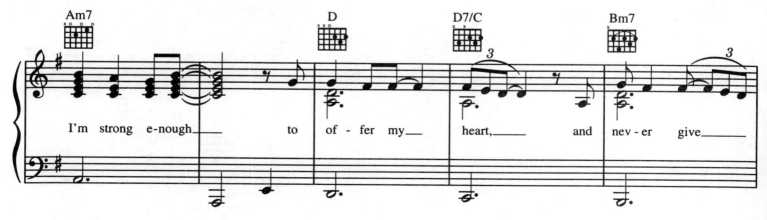

-ens that I'll nev-er_____ hold. But if dreams give you pow - er,_____ then

I'm strong e-nough_____ to of-fer my___ heart,_____ and nev-er give_____

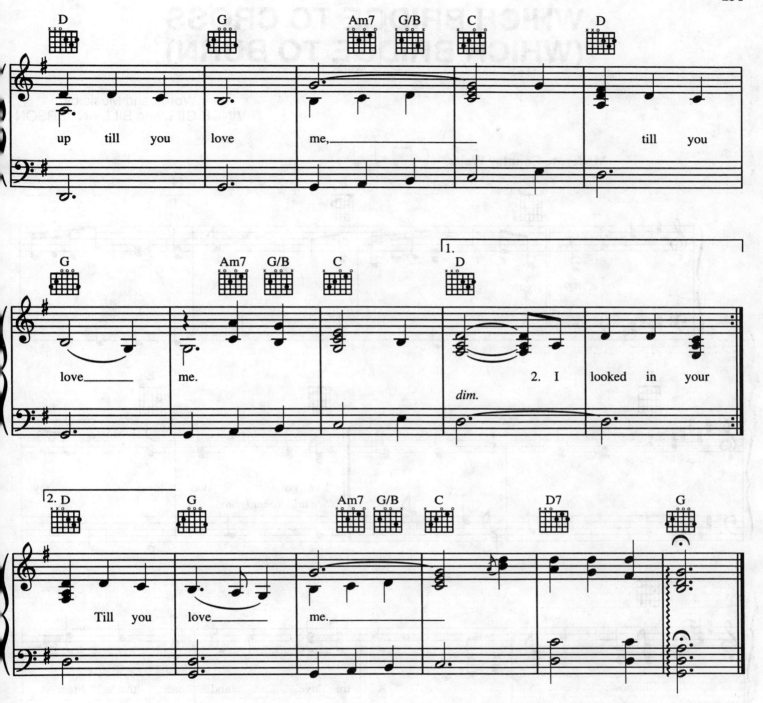

Verse 2:
I looked in your eyes, so bright and so blue.
And that's when I knew that you could be mine.
If good things come to those who wait,
Well, I guess I can wait if that's what I have to do.
Oh, it's worth it for you.
(To Chorus:)

WHICH BRIDGE TO CROSS
(WHICH BRIDGE TO BURN)

Words and Music by
VINCE GILL and BILL ANDERSON

254

Additional lyrics

2. I knew this was wrong, I didn't listen,
   A heart only knows what feels right.
   Oh, I need to reach a decision,
   And get on with the rest of my life.
   (To Chorus)